To Stephen –
Beyond this sign
is the
peek.

Long Long Ago

Peace Light & Love,
Shaun

LONG LONG AGO

Introductory quote from The Gift of Story by Clarissa Pinkola Estés, Ph.D. published by Ballantine Books, reprinted with written permission of RANDOM HOUSE, Inc.

For information address: **IMAGIC Unlimited** P.O. Box 230144 Portland, OR 97281-0144

FIRST EDITION
1st Printing

ISBN: 0-9636074-2-1
Library of Congress Catalog Card Number: 94-096536

Warren, Sharon.
Long long ago/by Sharon Warren. - 1st. ed.
p. cm.
Art and calligraphy by Elsie Petrequin.
ISBN 0-9636074-2-1:
1. Love - poetry, American. 2. New Thought - poetry.
I. Petrequin, Elsie. II. Title
PS3573.A77.L66 1995 94-96536
811'.54-dc20

Printed in THE UNITED STATES OF AMERICA
10 9 8 7 6 5 4 3 2
Printed on recycled paper

LONG LONG AGO

by Sharon Warren

Cover design by Elsie Petrequin
Art & Calligraphy by Elsie Petrequin

IMAGIC Unlimited - Oregon

"...that
which
they carried
within their hearts
had the most value, their
yearning and devotion ... And the
young couple here, like the Magi, were wise
too, for they gave the most golden of all things possible.
They gave their love, their truest love to one another.

from **THE GIFT OF STORY** by Dr. Clarissa Pinkola Estés

TO MY BELOVED KEITH

INTRODUCTION

Many of us have had the experience, at one time or another, of the feeling called *deja vu*. A feeling that we are experiencing an event we've had before, or meeting a person for the first time but having a sense that we know them.

The title poem, Long Long Ago, speaks of this KNOWING. It was written in November 1993 on the last leg of my flight from Portland, Oregon to my hometown in Michigan. As I seated myself in the small commuter plane, I quickly reached for my journal. Through the tears of remembrance, I recorded the words of the title poem, Long Long Ago.

This collection of poems, stories, "Angel Messages" and "Gems of Love" weave a tapestry of beauty and love. It is a love of two souls who have found each other once again. It is a true love that raises them to a higher level of awareness...conscious that the Spirit is the Source of all things. Love inspires, hopes, transforms, creates, transcends and dreams. Love is eternal. Love connects us to all beings, all creatures, and life.

Nearly everything in this book was recorded in my personal journals over the past two years. The "Gems of Love" are the words spoken to

me by my beloved. I recorded them in my journals to preserve his precious and beautiful words which are treasures for my soul. The "Angel Messages" came as profound insights which seemed to have significant meaning or guidance for me. I called them "Angel Messages" in my journals to remind me of the realm from which I felt they came.

I trust that you may find the joy of life inside you as you taste of the tender, succulent morsels of life that we share with you in **LONG LONG AGO.**

Author

ACKNOWLEDGEMENTS

My gratitude to **God**, all my **Angels, Guides** and **Teachers** for the inspiration, guidance and love that fills my life each day. To **Thelma Irene Gay Smith**, my Mother, for her abiding faith, constant love and emotional support...and for her Saturday morning phone calls over the 12 years since I left my Michigan home. To **Keith Johannessen**, my best friend, with deepest appreciation for editing the manuscript and for his inspiration, love and undying faith in me. Eternal gratitude for the "gems of love" he so freely shared with me and the world. To **Elsie Petrequin**, for the love, beauty and sensuality she brought to **LONG LONG AGO** through her art. To all my friends, too numerous to mention, for their love and encouragement. To **Roberta Jarrett, Steve Vaile, LaVon Richards, Colette DeWitt, Janet Holbrook and Jeanine Miller** for creative inspiration and the assurance, even through the darkest days, that "all-is-well". To **Carol Guthrie Sjolander** for her creative and meticulous graphic design skills, for the use of her office equipment, office space, and her positive attitude, love and constant support. To **Kadie Shrider** and **Patsy Cobb** for their outstanding abilities to slay the financial dragons of self-publishing. To **Bryan Stoneburner**, author of *Self-Publishing for Fun and Profit* for his new book which provided the additional information needed...just in time ...and for his Cataloging-in-Publication Data research. To **Murle Stillwagon Smith**, my beloved grandmother, for her spiritual presence with me. To **Dr. Wayne Dyer, Richard Bach, Dr. Deepak Chopra, Marianne Williamson, Rev. Mary Manin Morrissey**, my "teachers",

for *lighting the Way!!* To **Cris Ehlenfelt**, Crystal Wizard in Lincoln City, for providing a nurturing environment on the Oregon coast for me to rest and renew before publishing this book and for her love and support. To **Georgia Silva** for guiding us toward which poems, gems of love and angel messages "belonged" in this book...and for her love. Special thanks to John Hall for his sensitive portrait photography. To Pete Dorsett at Designer's Litho, much appreciation. Thanks to Bob Smith at Network Graphics, who printed our book, for his warmth, care and sensitivity to our very unique project. To Gary Walker and Spectrum West for the exquisite 4-color separations, to Wy'east Color for our black and white film processing and printing, to Rose City Bindery and to Oregon Laminations, Inc.

Other books by
Sharon Warren & Elsie Petrequin
ONE LIGHT ONE LOVE
ANGEL FINGERPRINTS: The Little Book of Joyous Thoughts

Relaxation Music Album
ONE LIGHT ONE LOVE, Vol. I
with Michael McCabe & Sharon Warren
For Information call (800) 945-4453

FOREWORD

There is a dream-like quality to this poetry, the fruit of a connection so deep that we are all included in its fullness. **Long Long Ago** is the touching call of love to know itself in which Sharon Warren opens her heart to meet yours. This book is a beautiful gift for the spirit, and I delight in its compelling innocence.

Alan Cohen, author of **The Dragon Doesn't Live Here Anymore**

CONTENTS I

CONTENTS II

Gems of Love

I am real
I am in you
And in your imagination
You are in me
And in my imagination.

SEARCHING SKIES

I soar high above
In the cool evening sky
I cry for my mate
Love's screams
Piercing the night.
Higher and higher
Alone I will fly
My heart filled with Love
Searching skies
For your sight.
Will you come?
Will you fly?
Hear my cry in the morn,
Know that I wait
Where the sun
And the sky's Love
Are born.

TRANSFORMATION

In anger I came
"Show me the way".
I cried in my heart
For answers to know.
Transformed I am here
To live in the truth
Beloved draw near.
In anger I see
Only separation and fear.
Live my desire
Only then will it come.
For now is the moment
Only Love will reveal,
No fault and no blame
Peaceful heart I am healed.

May all creation dance for joy within me. Dance for joy within me. Dance for joy... May all creation dance for joy within me. May all creation dance for joy within me.

FILLS WITH JOY

Thank you
For the smile
In your voice
For the truth
On your lips
For the Love
In your Soul
For the peace
In your touch
For the desire
In each breath
For the Light
In your heart
My world
Fills with joy
My life
In God's hands

Angel Messages

When two people share the same dreams---
those dreams come true.

COURAGE

On the deck
In morning light
A spider near
A web she weaves
Reminds me of
Your love, my Knight
As forth you thrust
To face your fear
To brush away
The scary beast
That crawled too near
My naked leg
In love you came
With heart of steel
To save your love
From fates unknown

No fiercer is
That spider, Love
Than dragons who
Are lurking near
The love within
Your heart and soul
Contains the power
That you will find
Your courage, strength
and knightly might
Flow from this love
And days of old
Go forth, my Knight
In Light of dawn
And know my heart
Waits your return
Stand in the Truth
Within your heart
In faith, in trust
The battle's won

A MIRACLE

Magical
Mystical
Love's pure delight
Dance in my Soul
Pristine fairy Light
Life pulses sweet
Eyes
Cannot see
Ears
Cannot hear
Hands
Cannot touch
Magical
Mystical
Miracle
Love

SWEET SOFTNESS

Sweet softness
Your love
Cradles my Soul
My heart
My life
Purely we love
In faith
And in trust
Sweet words
Velvet touch
Melt two hearts
Rise in flight
Heaven
On Earth

OH, I LOVE THE SEA

Oh, I love the sea
As true I love thee.
White foam
Kisses the sand
As your touch
Caresses my skin.
I breathe in the air
That, my Love, you have breathed.
The moon that you gaze upon
Shines down on me.
The stars in the heavens
Are the stars we both see.
The sun on my face
Shines also on thee.
My steps on the sand
Sound the beat of your heart.
Mother Earth, Father Sky,
You and I
One with all

were one the soul
below the sun
to where we are may
through space and time
our souls have flown
to find the love we knew
two hearts, two minds
two spirits dance
as one, for ever may
now feel the power
the dance
is all here in

TWO SPIRITS DANCE

We've come so far
Beyond the sun
To where we are today
Through space and time
Our souls have flown
To find the love we knew
Two hearts, two minds
Two spirits dance
In life's eternal play
Sing on, Sweet Love
Now feel the power
God's Love
Is all there is.

THE TRUTH OF LOVE

I thought you'd gone
But you were here
Outside my aching heart.
I cried alone inside my mind,
My heart o'ercome with fear.
In quietness of forest green
Beside the brook I sat.
To feel and know
The Peace of God,
Inside my weary heart.
The Truth of Love
It never fails
Tho' wander far we may.
Just go inside, it's always there
To heal our dark despair.

UNTIL

Until you come home
I will sleep
With the memory
Of your arms
Warm around me
Your heart beating near
The sound of your breathing
The Love in your Soul
Alone in my bed
Not alone in my heart
Until you return

SACRIFICE OF LOVE

My Beloved, I offer you up to The Creator, my sacrifice of Love. I place you in the hands of God. I release you to fly free. I see the precious you that you have always been. I celebrate the beautiful you that you are becoming...a butterfly emerging from the darkness...a Phoenix rising from the ashes. My grateful heart stands in awe at the throne of God, knowing that you are protected. I set you free to feel the wind beneath your wings, that you may feel the magnificence of the power and love that you are. If it be God's will, I pray that one day we may forever fly together in the same sky and share the vision of new horizons, new worlds beyond the stars. May our love be the fuel to take us there...two gentle beings...come so far from who we were to who we are today. Oh God, purify me, sanctify me in the fire of life, that I may one day fly again to Heaven's door in sight of my Heart's Desire, My Beloved. May we rest our wings beside the still waters of your Love...home again.

LOVE'S FLAME

Dear Angels,
Fly
From this heart;
Bear Love's flame
Beyond the stars
To my love's
Own true Self;
Bridge rainbow light
Two Souls
To bind
With God's
Pure grace
Sweet passion
Tell

Angel Messages

Life can be magic;
Life can be tragic;
It's your choice--
What are you going
to make of it?

FAREWELL

Farewell
My sweet Love
Let not desire
Hold you back.

For you
Hold the key
To the doors of
All your dreams.

May you find
Who you are
What you want
Where to go.

Walk on Love's
Light strewn path
Safe and warm
Evermore

ON FOREST TRAIL

Oh…That I could share
This day with you
Green of life
Life renews
Path once walked
Now
Again
Peace-filled heart
Shines on through
Love is new
You are here
In my soul
In my mind
In my heart
We are One
Love's true Light
Web of Life
Catch my dreams
See them grow

Angel Messages

Keep the Light of this Love burning!
Don't ever let it die through fear, doubt or anger.
Keep it alive!

MY LOVE WILL TAKE YOU HOME

I will make a bed for you
Beneath the apple tree
A place where you can rest awhile
I'll be waiting there for thee.
The grass so sweet upon your skin
Beneath the starry sky
I'll lie beside you till the dawn
My dreams with you will fly
Your soul, with mine, to Heaven shall soar
For in that night of dream-filled sleep
In arms of love, you're safe and warm
In Love's celestial peace
The smell of blossoms, sounds of night
Entwine two hearts as one
For in this time of love-filled bliss
We find the peace we've won.
Sweet Prince of Love, I wait for you
My heart safe in your hands
When battle's done and dragon's slain
One Love will rule the land.

COMMUNION

Communion in the Light
Love around
Christ within
Willing to hear
Willing to see
Rejoice in the Earth
Rise all toward
One Light
Love within
Evermore

Gems of Love

You are going to do fine.
I believe in you.
My heart is with you.

WILL YOU...

Will you come to me
In my dreams
And hold me 'til the dawn?
Will you wrap your arms
Around me
Until I fall asleep?
Will you be with me
Each blessed night
'Til we're together again?
Will you be with me
And love me true
No matter where you are?
Will you kiss my cheek
As I awake
Although we're miles apart?
Will you dry my tears
As I wait, my Love,
To be with you again?

SWEET LOVE'S SPIRIT

Sweet one
  Sweet love
    Sweet voice
      In the night

Sound of one
  Sound of love
    Sounds so sweet
      Love in flight

I'm awake
  Though I sleep
    I'm asleep
      Though awake

In Love's sea
  Spirits float
    In sweet peace
      Ever safe

WELCOME HOME

How would I find you
Through space and through time
I'd know by your way
Your love and your voice
No matter how far
You'd come to my side
The way that you move
Would stir feelings inside
So long, long ago
Apart we were torn
To drift on through time
To places unknown
One day we'd come back
To all that we've known
And awaken the memory
Of the Love that we've sown
Through darkness we've wandered
Through eternity
To find what we'd lost
Welcome home...we are here.

Angel Messages

Harness your sexual energy...
direct it toward creative efforts
and you will change the world.

THOUGHTS OF YOU

I feel
Vibrations
As I lie here
Alone
Thoughts of you
Dreams of two
Ecstasy known
I feel you
We rise again
Light
Of my Soul
Love
It is all

FOREVER UNITED

Only the illusion
Of time and space
Separates our
Two hearts
That beat as One.
Forever united
In eternal Love.
Through darkness
We struggle
To find the
Light of God.

LOVE IS A FLOWER

If one forces a flower to open before its time, one destroys its beauty. Everything must unfold in its own time. We must be observers in God's Garden, enjoying the wonder of each display, each in its own season with its unique and glorious gift.....Oh, that we humans would remember! For in picking at each flower to hasten its opening, we only bruise and tatter the delicate petals and destroy the possibility of the sweet fragrance that can only come in its time. And would we allow ourselves the same nurturing patience...to observe our own unfolding into the full and magnificent radiance that we are becoming...to stop picking at ourselves and only observe the beauty of who we are...at each stage of our own development...from seed to plant to bud to blossom and to seed again. An endless circle of growth and unfolding. Each metamorphosis, another beautiful miracle in our progress

of becoming. Only, as the loving observer, do we see the true beauty of each period of our life as another stepping stone on the miraculous journey in the circle of life. What appears to be death or loss is only transformation to another NEW BEGINNING....and the circle never ends... Rejoice in the journey! Rejoice in the unfolding! Find peace and joy as an observer in this beautiful garden....as the observer of your own graceful opening up to the Light...and as the observer of the development and magnificence of all the other flowers in God's Garden.

YOU HAVE THE POWER

Love of my life
Dream of my dreams
Walk through the darkness
Come home to me.

Love 'waits you here
When battle is done
Fierce dragons o'ercome
Slay them, my Love.

You have the Power
It flows through you now
Courage and might
To open the door.

Now is the time
Now is the hour
You are a King
My heart you have won.

NATURE'S PEACE

Warm spring sun
Peaceful and calm
Trees and birds
Ground squirrels and jays
Woodpeckers and crows
Sunshine and trees
Communion with all
God's Presence we feel
Love's Light grows around
Heals our hearts
And the World
Home we've come
Not alone
Peace within
Light the World

LONG LONG AGO

Who were we before...
When did we love,
That now we have found
The peace we knew then?

Were you a great warrior,
Courageous and strong?
Did I silently wait
'Til your journey was o'er?

Did I trust in you then
As, in faith, I do now
And wait by the fire
Until your return?

Did I love you
And care for
Your needs
And your home?

Is the passion that burns
In my heart and my Soul
Born of the days
So long, long ago?

Oh, the heart of this maiden
Overflows with sweet peace...
Begun from the tears
Sprung from Great Spirit's Love.

Did you hold me and caress
My dark maiden's skin?
Did I carry your children
And fill your desires?

Did we walk by the rivers
And lie in the grass?
Were there laughter and tears?
Were we happy as now?

Great Spirit has blessed us
With nature's sweet Love.
May we love on forever
No beginning...no end.

I LOVE YOU

I see
Your Soul
    Light of
        All life...I love you.

I see
Your form
    Your flaws
        Your fears...I still love you.

I know
Your strengths
    Your weaknesses
        Too...And I love you.

I watch
I wait
    God's will
        Be done...I love you.

ALONE

Alone,
But not alone
Feeling you near
Knowing you're here
Dreaming
Watching you sleep
In the light
Of the dawn
I lie
By your side
Like a child
You awaken
A kiss and a smile
Your arms
Wrap around me
One more day
To love you
And to pray
For the day
You will be here

LOVE IS

Sand, sun
Surf sounds
Blue sky
Two by two
Now three
Now four
Each loving
Sand, sea and sky
Alone I sit
Nay, not alone
And watch
The dance of life
Around
To be is peace
Love heals
Love is

TWO FORKS OF THE CREEK

Two forks of the creek...both different...both the same...separate energy from two sources...but really from one ultimate Source...meet, join and blend to create a larger more powerful force for change.

GOLDEN RAYS

Golden rays
Beyond the dawn
Transcend this world
Of tears and pain
For Love waits there
Where hearts are free
To love in Light
Above the wind
Souls' music blends
Two hearts as One
Sweet peace
Sweet Love

WE ARE LOVE

In that realm
Of Beyond
Between sleep
And awake
I hear your sweet voice
Speaking words--
Of this world
They are not;
And only have meaning
On a heavenly plane.
My heart
Understands:
"I am with you
 In that place
 Where time
         ...and space
                 ...don't exist"
We are Love.

Angel Messages

Listen with your Heart...not your mind, your emotions, your body, your ears, or your eyes!

I WAIT

I am the shore
You are the sea
Power and beauty
Returning ever
To my feet
Cleansing my soul
Laying gifts
In my hands
Endlessly leaving
Promised return
I wait
Firm and wet
For the love
Longing knows
On and on
Evermore

Gems of Love

I will miss you very much.
Know that I'll be with you.
Feel my presence every night.
I love you.

IMAGES

Sunshine
  Trees
    Warmth

Birds
  Mountains
    Wild flowers

Love
  Sharing
    Laughter

Peace
  Wonder
    Gratitude

Quiet
  Water
    Peace

GOOD MORNING, SUNSHINE

"Good morning, Sunshine"
Sweet and pure
His voice is radiant
Filled with love
My heart is light
It now has wings
To fly beyond
The clouds, the rain
The wind, the sun
Two hearts, two minds
Two souls now One

SOON

"Soon"
Blessed "soon"
I know
What you mean
No space
And no time
Only Eternity
Want
And desire
True Love
Peace of mind
Forever
Together
We are One
You and I

F aith
E cstasy
E mergence
L ove
 I magination
No end
God
S erenity

BEYOND FOREVER

Hear the songs
Inside my head
That sing the sound
Of passion's dream
That tell of Love
So sweet, so dear
That only choirs
Of Angels sing
Notes drift through
Souls' enchanted land
To blend two hearts
As One
Beyond forever
We have come
Forever Home
We fly
For in the realm
Of Spirit's peace
Together
Now, we are.

TAKE MY HAND

Take my hand
Walk beside me
Toward the Light
Beyond the Sun
Love waits there
To take us Home
One pure Light
Where all are One
Peace and joy
Beyond the pain
God's true Promise
In His hands

RE-UNION

The day you appeared
I knew who you were
A friend and a lover
From long, long ago.

Returned from a journey
We'd travelled so far
Searching and hoping
Souls following their hearts.

A lifetime we wandered
This earth in a dream
Longing and craving
But not knowing why.

Life's trek led us here
Heavenly rapture returns
In our minds, in our hearts
Love's fulfilled... We are One.

SHIP OF LOVE

I touch your Light
My being glows
Each breath, my life
Through yours revealed.
Sweet rapture flows
Between two souls
Now found the Love
They've always known.
Transformed in Light
Through Love's pure bliss
    Sail on
        One mast
            Two sails.

THE RAIN

The gentle rain
Falls on my ear
As I recall
The memory of
Your loving touch
Clean and fresh
The rain
Your love

I WONDER

I wonder
How many times
How many lives
Through eons of years
Have we made Love
Not enough
He replies
Never the same
Always new
Always free
I've loved you forever
I will eternally
Your strength
And your haven
Safe and warm
You will be
Love flows on in time
Dance of Life
You and me

Angel Messages

When making Love becomes a sacrament,
A testimony to the Glory of God,
We are in Heaven.

LITTLE SQUIRREL

Little squirrel
Little friend
Share the sun
Now with me
Scratch and roll
In the sand
Unafraid
Not alone
You and me
We are free
We are loved
We are One

WHERE ARE YOU

Where are you, my Love?
I feel you so near
Through time and through space
My heart waits to hear

The sound of your voice
The Love in your soul
We drift on forever
Through darkness and cold

The warmth of our Love
The flame we can't hide
A beacon that guides us
To Heaven on high

ONLY LOVE IS REAL

Our love is growing more beautiful each passing day as I let go and allow it freedom to blossom…I focus on the beauty of the essence of its truth…not what the "world" thinks…nor what my eyes see…nor what my ears hear…that is illusion. Only <u>Love</u> is <u>Real</u>. Our relationship exists to serve God.

WAND OF MAGIC

Wand of Magic
Feel the Power
Pulsing Light
Transform this hour
Two travel forth
Beyond the stars
True hearts
And minds
As One
Now fly

YOU ARE HERE

By the window
'Neath the bridge
I see the sight
Your eyes have seen.
Your spirit blends
With sea and sky
Soft peace and love
Flow through my soul.
Calm coolness laps
At stone-strewn sand
Where once your feet
Left dimpled kisses.
I love this place
That you have loved
And know you're here
Tho' miles away.

SWEET LOVE'S REWARD

Beyond the moon
Beyond the stars
Beyond this moment
There we are
Catch your dreams
Bring them home
Wrapped in my Love
Dream's magic spins
Sweet Love's reward

Gems of Love

I cannot imagine
 Heaven being more beautiful
 Than this very moment
 As my being fills
  With the essence of you.

FLY FREE

I leave you now
For I must fly
Beyond the clouds
To Heaven on high.
I spread my wings
And feel the wind
Flow through me
Lift me up.
I am Light
I feel the sun
As higher I soar
Toward realms unknown.
My heart will always
Love you
Know you
I fly free
We both are free.

COME TO ME

When you are free
Come to me
Fly to me
My heart waits
In my dreams
For the day
You fly free
Abiding Love
Faith and trust
Waits in peace
Come to me

ONE LOVE

Together
As One
Bodies melding
Soul and mind
Transcends
One
Light enfolds
One with God
Pure Love
Pure Light
No Beginning
And no end
Drift on
Journey through
The night
To the stars
And beyond
One Love

ONE WITH ALL

We are One
With the stars
With the Earth
And the seas
Dolphins, whales
Birds and trees
One with all
You and me
Wondrous life
Shared by all
Truth and Light
Me and thee

IN CLOUDS OF WHITE

In clouds of white
I see your face
The rain, my tears
Whene'er you're gone.
The breeze, your touch
My heart to calm.
The sun, your smile
To warm my Soul.
I wait to hear
Your loving voice.
Not words but sounds
Your heart I hear.
Birds sing, your laughter
I am healed.

MY SONG

Heart swells
Mind soars
Now I'm
With you
Stars glow
Moon knows
Our Love
Shines through
Soul sees
One dream
Two fly
Into blue
My song
Heart's Love
Pledged now
To you

DANCE THE DREAM

I hold him
Near in my Soul
This man
Of my dreams
Love pulsing
Through my veins
Electricity of Life
Music of Heaven
Dance the dream
Of the past
Walk beside me
Light of Light
Once again
He brings me Love
To feed my Soul

Angel Messages

As I find my way,
I light the way for others.

DANCE WITH THE FIRE

Dance with the Fire
Walk on the coals
One with the Fire
Earth, wind and rain.
Join with the fear
See Oneness in all
Rise from the flames
From the ashes below.
Transformed in the Light
Phoenix rising again.
Born again, I am free
Freedom's passion now won.

YOUR EYES

Your eyes
Speak truth
Of Love
To me
Your eyes
Say more
Than words
Can say
Be still
My mind
Those eyes
Don't lie
Soul Speaks
Through eyes
Of Love

LOVE SUSTAINS

Nothing
  Not parents
    Not job
      Not circumstances
Can keep us apart
The Love that we are
We have always been
It transcends all the pain
And challenges we face
On this Earth Walk
This Love sustains us
On life's turbulent waters
It calms the seas
And brings blessed Peace
Of the Holy Spirit
To all that
We touch

REST YOUR HEART ON MY SHORE

Sail on through the storm
Tho' the journey be long
My love waits to hold you
My heart is your home

My love is your beacon
Sail on through the night
Light of love, it will guide you
Safely home to my sight

There, in peace, I will hold you
Rest your heart on my shore
Warm sunshine surround you
Taste sweet love, evermore

TAPESTRY OF LIFE

I savor the memories of yesterday and live in the now of my existence, knowing that only your physical body has departed from my touch, yet our hearts beat as one. Our minds and souls have never, will never, walk alone. We are woven together so beautifully as we create this wondrous tapestry called life...light and darkness...all colors of the rainbow, from the yellow sunshine of our laughter to the soft blue of our tears. Apart and together, each creating through the ever-winding thread, this intricate and lovely blanket of life. Only Love shall make this vision a pattern to cherish all our days...memories we hold in our hearts throughout eternity. Let the Heavens dance between us for that is the silence which allows the notes of our song to be heard.

Sharon Warren, author, poet and publisher was born and raised in rural Michigan, where her love of life and nature are deeply rooted with her Native American ancestry. Sharon received her B.S. from Central Michigan University in 1967 and moved to the Pacific Northwest in 1982. Writing and creating books since childhood, she has been guided by Spirit to create and publish

Photo by John Hall

beautiful and unique gift books of poetry and inspirational thoughts from her own personal journals. This treasury of beautiful messages warms the heart and inspires Love and Hope. In collaboration with her long-time friend, Elsie Petrequin, **LONG LONG AGO** is, like their first book, **ONE LIGHT ONE LOVE**, a unique collection of Love-inspired poems, with artistry to capture the essence of romance and life's wonder. **ANGEL FINGERPRINTS**, a collection of joyous thoughts, is their latest.

Elsie Petrequin, artist, calligrapher, and educator has reached higher levels than ever before in her current work in **LONG LONG AGO**. Her sensitivity, love of life and ability to tap in to a Higher Source to translate the poetry and prose of Sharon Warren in a sensuous, magical way touches the hearts of all who observe her talents. Ms. Petrequin attained her B.S. in

Art at Portland State University and her M.S. with Honors in Art Teaching from the University of Oregon. Ms. Petrequin's career is continuing to expand in the direction of book illustration, book and CD cover design, watercolor/calligraphic art, and original design-work for companies around the Pacific Northwest. With the guidance of Spirit, she explores ever new realms of expression through her "dancing fingers".